Love is a LAUGH

EDITED BY

MARGARET GREENMAN

WITH ILLUSTRATIONS BY

WENDY WATSON

THE PETER PAUPER PRESS

Mount Vernon · New York

Love Is a Laugh

Love Is a Laugh

———◆———

COMING home very very late one night, Adam found Eve waiting angrily.

"Late again," she pouted. "You must be seeing some other woman."

"I consider that accusation wildly absurd," shouted the outraged Adam. "You know perfectly well that you and I are quite alone in this world."

With this, Adam retired for the night. Something soon caused him to awake with a start. There, hovering over him, was Eve — painstakingly counting his ribs.

———◆———

Honey was happily displaying her engagement ring to her friends.

"It's a boy," she chirped. "Six feet tall and weighs 190 pounds."

A young groom came upon his bride fussing in the tiny kitchen of their apartment.

"What's the matter, honey?" he asked.

"Darling," his love wailed, "I rinsed the ice cubes in this hot water and now I can't find them!"

Tammy and a friend were discussing Tammy's new husband.

"George and I have an understanding," Tammy explained. "He goes his way, and I go with him. . . ."

She was quite swept away when her boy-friend offered her an engagement ring.

"Oh, darling," she cried, "this is so sudden, at last!"

A young man who had great difficulty in speaking to girls suddenly amazed his friends with the announcement that he was engaged. One friend asked how it happened.

"Well," said the bashful fellow, "I danced with her three times and I couldn't think of anything else to say."

The young husband was trying to persuade his bride to come swimming with him in the sea. She refused to dive in; it was much too cold.

Gravely he gathered some sticks from the beach, started a bonfire, borrowed a kettle, boiled some water in it, and then poured the water into the Atlantic.

Whereupon his wife dove right in.

The honeymooners were strolling in the evening beside the ocean. The groom, moved by the beauty of the scene, recited, "Roll on, thou deep and lingering waves, roll on."

His bride gazed out over the sea for a while and then turned to her husband in amazement. "Why, you marvelous man. They're doing it!"

"Katie, I hear that you are going to Hawaii with your husband. Aren't you nervous about such a long flight?"

"Well, that's James' lookout. I belong to him now, and if anything happens to me, it'll be his loss, not mine."

Tom was showing Suzy how to use a wishbone.

"We must both make a wish and pull," he explained.

"But I do not know what to wish for," she protested.

"But surely you can think of something."

"No," she replied, "I can't think of anything I want very much."

"Well, I'll wish for you!"

"You'll really wish for me?" the delighted Suzy asked. "Well, then, there's no use bothering with the old wishbone. You can have me!"

Girl to rather homely, unassuming suitor: "I'm probably very fond of you, Herbert — but I hate to admit it to myself."

A young girl and her mother were discussing their favorite topic.

"What do you give a man who has everything?" asked the neophyte.

"Encouragement."

A pretty young lady in Ohio had a persistent but undesired suitor in New York. He pressed an ardent campaign for her hand through the mails, sending a special delivery letter twice a day for sixty-three days. On the sixty-fourth day the campaign produced results.

The girl ran off with the mailman.

"Oh, Jane — that gorgeous lifeguard finally noticed me!"

"How do you know?"

"Well, he just flexed a smile at me!"

A certain railway in Michigan has a station called Sawyer's Mills, or Sawyer, for short.

A young rural couple on one of the trains attracted much attention by evident fondness for each other. Finally the brakeman thrust his head in the doorway of the car and called out, "Sawyer! Sawyer!"

At once the young man of the couple jumped up indignantly and exclaimed, "Well, I don't care if you did — we've been engaged three weeks."

An intensely bashful fellow was driving one evening with a young lady whom he'd been seeing for some time. The stillness of the evening and the beauty of the scene around him inspired his courage. Sitting stiffly erect and with his face forward, he asked suddenly, "May I kiss you?"

"Surely," his love coyly replied.

"Aw," he said, his face scarlet, and stepping on the accelerator, "aw, I was only fooling."

During the war a nurse in the Philippines fell in love with an officer patient, and they planned to marry the day he was released from the hospital. Not wishing to be married in her khaki uniform, she got permission to wear a wedding gown.

After the ceremony the overwhelmed groom announced to all, "Isn't she lovely? This is the first time I've ever seen her with a dress on!"

"Isn't he handsome?" the excited bride exclaimed. "It's the first time I've seen him when he wasn't in pajamas!"

The young lover had finally gotten up the courage to ask his darling to marry him, and anxiously awaited her reply.

"Dearest," she said, "before I give you my answer you must tell me something. Do you drink anything?"

A smile of relief lighted his face. Was that all she wanted to know? Proudly, triumphantly, he clasped her in his arms and whispered, "Anything!"

"Lucy, my dearest, I adore you more than mere words can ever say . . ."

"But, darling, don't ever let that discourage you from trying!"

Lydia had just received a long awaited engagement ring. Much to her disappointment, none of her friends at the office noticed it. Finally, unable to stand it a moment longer, she exclaimed, "Oh, dear — I'm so warm in my new ring!"

An optimist is a fellow who, upon discovering that he forgot his wife's birthday, assumes that she forgot it too.

At the airport a flustered young bridegroom starting on his honeymoon absent-mindedly asked for one ticket to the Bahamas. But when his wife pointed out his error, he answered without a moment's hesitation, "By thunder, you're right, dear! I'd forgotten myself completely."

———◆———

"What are you so sad about this evening, honeybunch?"

"Oh, George, love, I was thinking that this would be our last evening together, until tomorrow night."

———◆———

"Am I the first girl you ever kissed?" she asked.

"That's quite possible," he replied. "Were you in Kansas City in 1957?"

———◆———

The youthful Mrs. Boggs sat plying her needle. A coat of her husband's was in her lap. As her husband appeared, she said fretfully, "It's terrible, the careless way clothes are made these days. This is the fifth time I've had to sew this button back on for you!"

Sally, just recently wed, entered the dining room and proudly placed a turkey on the table.

"There you are, my love, our first Thanksgiving turkey!"

Her husband gazed at the bird with hungry admiration. "Wonderful, darling," he said. "How beautifully you have stuffed it!"

"Stuffed!" she echoed. "But, honey, this one wasn't hollow!"

———◆———

Scientist Seth was watching his wife cook supper.

"What's that strange looking dish?" he asked.

"Well, dear, it's an experiment," she replied.

"O.K., love, I'll have the control."

———◆———

Helen was discussing her latest beaux with a friend.

"If I could combine their qualities, I'd be the happiest girl in the world. James is clever, rich, handsome, and debonaire. Clarence wants to marry me."

This couple had been happily married for years, but one morning at breakfast the wife was obviously in a very bad mood.

"What's the trouble?" her husband asked.

At first she did not want to tell, but finally she turned to him and blurted out, "If I ever dream again that you kissed another woman, I'll never speak to you as long as I live!"

On a quiet evening at home, a wife suggested to her husband, "Dear, why don't you read to me while I sew?"

The husband obviously was uneasy at the idea, stammered a bit, then replied, "I tell you what — you sew to me while I read."

Girl to her date in a night club: "Goodness, I think I'll have another drink. It makes you so witty!"

You can't kiss a girl unexpectedly — only sooner than she thought you would.

The wife of a young engineer, off on a job in Iceland, knitted him a warm jacket which she air-mailed with the following letter:

"Postage costs so much for every little ounce that I have cut off the buttons. Love and kisses.

"P.S. The buttons are in the right-hand pocket."

As a gift for his wife, a Senator visiting the Far East bought a beautiful and exotic medallion. His wife wore it proudly to a number of public functions, until the evening when a Chinese diplomat informed her gravely that the Chinese characters on the medallion read, "Licensed prostitute, City of Shanghai."

"But, darling," said the sweet young thing, "if I marry you, I'll lose my job."

"We could keep our marriage a secret, couldn't we?" asked the eager young man.

"But suppose we have a baby?"

"Oh, we'd tell the baby, of course."

"For goodness sake, use both hands," shrilled the co-ed in the auto.

"I can't," replied her escort. "I have to steer with one."

One fellow decided that his sweetheart really ought to learn to love the national pastime. However, due to her tardiness they arrived at the ball park when the game was well into the fifth inning.

As they walked to their seats, the sweet young thing heard a fan remark that the score was nothing to nothing.

"Oh, good," she cooed to her escort. "Then we haven't missed a thing!"

A young girl, taken somewhat aback by such names as "Temptation" and "My Sin," inquired of the salesgirl:

"Haven't you got something for — a beginner?"

"Am I really the only girl you've ever kissed?" she asked.

"Certainly — and by far the prettiest."

The young lovers, trying to find a secluded spot for a long embrace, found people, people, people everywhere. Suddenly the man had an idea and he led the girl to the railway station. Standing beside the door of a car as though seeing her off, he kissed her fondly. After the couple had repeated the experiment at four or five different platforms, a sympathetic porter strolled up and whispered to the young man, "Why don't you take her around to the bus terminal? They go every three minutes from there."

Young Henry was very bashful in the presence of the fair sex. His parents were therefore surprised and pleased when he announced that he was going downtown to see a young lady.

One hour later he was back, breathing heavily and flushed with excitement.

"Well," asked the parents, "didn't you see the girl after all?"

"Oh, I sure did see her," replied Henry enthusiastically, "and if I hadn't ducked pretty quickly up an alley, she would have seen me!"

22

One day a famous movie millionaire, about to board a friend's yacht, saw a slip of a girl standing on the edge of the wharf.

"For some inexplicable reason," he recalls, "I had an uncontrollable impulse to push her into the water. To my horror — I did. I had no idea if she could swim. I expected an infuriated young woman. Instead, she came to the surface, blinked the water out of her eyes and smiled a brilliant smile.

"By God!" I said to myself, "that's the girl I'm going to marry."

And he did.

———◆———

George Bernard Shaw was for once taken aback when he appealed to Mrs. Shaw for support of his claim that male judgment was superior to female judgment.

"Of course, dear," replied Mrs. Shaw. "After all, you married me and I you."

———◆———

A platonic friendship may be defined as the interval between the introduction and the first kiss.

A lovely girl was shopping along Fifth Avenue when she noticed that she was being followed by a smooth Latin type.

After a while she turned on him, indignant.

"You've been following me for three blocks — I saw you. You can stop right now. I'm not the type of girl you can pick up."

The Latin bowed, and smiled. "Madame," he said, "I am not picking you up. I am picking you *out*."

It worked!

———◆———

An Indian happened to be sending smoke signals to his girl at the time of a large nuclear test in Nevada. Gazing into the sky at the huge mushroom cloud, the Indian was stunned for a moment. Then he was heard to mutter, "Gosh, I wish I'd said that!"

———◆———

"I really don't ask much in life," said the pretty young thing. "All I want is a nice man to love and understand me. Is that too much to expect of a millionaire?"

24

"Say, pal, how'd you enjoy your vacation trip?"

"Fine, fine. My wife did all the driving."

"Then I guess you had a chance to enjoy the scenery?"

"Yes, all I had to do was hold the wheel."

"No, I never was exactly disappointed in love," the attractive young bachelor explained. "I was more what you might call discouraged.

"You see, when I was very young I fell in love with a girl, but I was mortally afraid to tell her of my feelings. At last I summoned my courage to the proposing point, and said, 'Let's get married.'

" 'Good Lord!' exclaimed my love in reply, 'who'd have us?' "

Solomon's 777th wife asked, "Sol, are you really and truly in love with me?"

"My dear, you are one in a thousand."

Happily she snuggled closer.

Sixteen-year-old Nancy was entertaining one of her latest beaux. The fellow happened to remark while Nancy's mother was in the room that he had come from Brooklyn. Making conversation, the mother explained that she and Nancy's father had lived there eighteen years ago, when they were first married. Whereupon, a startled expression passed over the young people's faces.

Next morning, Nancy explained with disgust, "Well, Mother, that certainly did it. I'd told him I was eighteen; so then of course I had to tell him that I was illegitimate."

———◆———

The young lady gazed fondly at her new engagement ring.

"Is it a real diamond?" she asked.

"If it isn't, I got taken for half a dollar."

———◆———

"You're really a very pretty girl."

"Now, now," she blushed. "You'd say so even if you didn't think so."

"Sure, but you'd think so even if I didn't say so."

The luggage-carrying husband stared miserably down the tracks after the departing train.

"If you hadn't taken so long getting ready," he admonished his wife, "we would have caught it."

"Yes," his wife rejoined, "and if you hadn't hurried me so, we wouldn't have to wait for the next one!"

———————

"Now I know that love-making is just the same as it always was."

"How is that?"

"Well, I just read about a Greek maiden who sat and listened to a lyre all evening."

———————

Said the meek little man as he surveyed the florist's wares, "I'd like something in the nature of a peace feeler for my wife."

———————

She: "Do you know why I won't marry you?"

He: "I can't think."

She: "Oh, you guessed it right away."

27

"I'm in charge of the office today," said the middle-aged woman. "What can I do for you?"

The farmer hesitated.

"You sure this is the Woman's Exchange?"

"Of course."

"And you're the woman?"

"That's right. What can I do for you?"

"Nothin'," said the farmer. "I guess I'll keep Semanthy, after all."

He: "Dearest, I must marry you."

She: "Have you seen Father and Mother?"

He: "Often, darling; but I love you anyway."

Following a broken engagement, the enraged young lady sent back all of the lad's letters, marked, "Fourth Class Male."

In the spring a young man's fancy lightly turns to what a girl has been thinking about all winter.

She stood at the counter, an obviously new bride, while a clerk explained various household gadgets to her. He explained enthusiastically that an electrically timed egg cooker would make sure that her husband's eggs were just right every morning.

"But I wouldn't need that," she said. "John likes his eggs the way I do them. I just look out the window at the traffic light, give them one red and two greens, and they're done."

———

The father's tone of voice was severe.

"Young man," he said, "do you think you should be taking my daughter to night clubs all the time?"

"Certainly not!" the boy answered, then added hopefully, "let's try to reason with her."

———

One psychiatrist was very happily married to a surprisingly ugly woman.

"I know she's terribly homely," he explained to a friend, "and somewhat cross-eyed, and a bit dull — but what nightmares she has!"

A hillbilly had been courting a mountain girl. At last her father spoke up, "You've been seeing Nellie for nigh onto a year. What are your intentions — honorable or dishonorable?"

The startled young blood replied, "You mean I got a choice?"

"What would you say if I asked you to marry me?"

"Nothing. I can't talk and laugh at the same time."

"Is the steak ready now, dear?" inquired the new husband.

"Not yet, I'm afraid. It looked hopeless grilled, and it doesn't look much better fried, but if you'll be patient a little longer, I'll see what boiling does to it."

"I've been asked to get married plenty of times," said the country girl with a toss of her head.

"Who asked yuh, Daisy?" inquired her boy friend.

"Oh, Pa and Ma."

A British aristocrat once married a delightful blonde from the Music Hall chorus. Their life together was happy but uneventful until an art gallery exhibited a life-sized portrait of the young lady in the altogether.

Attempting to placate her enraged husband, the girl explained, "Believe me, you have nothing to be angry about. He did it from memory."

"The marvelous thing about being a stewardess," remarked one young lady to another, "is that you meet so many eligible fellows, and they're all strapped down!"

"They do say," he began hesitantly, "that kisses are the language of love."

"Well," his love coyly replied, "speak for yourself, John."

"What do you mean by bringing my daughter home at three o'clock in the morning?" stormed the angry father.

"Well, sir, I have to be at work at seven."

"Dottie, your boy friend seems very timid," said Mama. "Why don't you encourage him a bit?"

"Encourage him!" her daughter replied. "He cannot take the clearest hint. Only last night, when I sat alone on a sofa and he perched across the room on a chair, I remarked on the oddity that a man's arm and a girl's waist seem always to be the same length. Can you imagine what he did then?"

"Why, just as any man would — he tried it."

"Wrong — he asked me if I could find a piece of string so we could take a measure."

———————◆———————

"Betsy, didn't I tell you not to have that man over to your apartment?" said Mama. "You know how I worry."

"But, Mama — I went over to his apartment. Now let *his* mother do the worrying!"

———————◆———————

"Is the canned ham all right, dear?" asked the anxious bride.

"Marvelous! Did you slice it yourself?"

"If I refuse to be your wife," she whispered dramatically, "will you really commit suicide?"

"That," he said grandly, "has been my usual procedure."

It happened in London during an air-raid. The girl said, " 'Erbert, you really shouldn't 'ave kissed me like that, with all those people so close around us, even if it was in the dark."

"I didn't kiss you," said the boy, looking angrily around in the crowd. "I only wish I knew who it was—I'd teach 'im."

" 'Erbert," sighed the girl, "you couldn't teach 'im nothing."

A New Hampshire farmer had been urged to attend the funeral of his neighbor's third wife. "But I'm not goin'," he announced to his own wife.

"Goodness sakes, why not?" she asked.

"Well, Mary, I'm beginnin' to feel kinda awkward about goin' so often without anything of the sort to ask him back to."

34

The Reverend H. P. Jones had just married a young couple, and the bridegroom asked him the price of the service.

"Oh, well," said the minister, "you can pay me whatever it is worth to you."

The young fellow looked long and silently at his bride. Then, turning wonderingly to the minister he replied, "You have ruined me for life, then — you really have."

"Well, Willie, what does your sister think of the engagement ring I gave her?"

"Aw, she says the other two cost more."

"Darling, did you really paint that silo?" asked Sam's admiring sweetheart from the city.

"Why, sure."

"By hand?" she asked wonderingly again.

"Yep."

"Well, think of that — a hand-painted silo!"

The essence of true love was discovered in a brief conversation between a young man and a very pretty girl.

"And you're very sure you love me?" she asked.

"Love you?" echoed the young fellow. "Why, darling, while I was kissing you good-night on the porch last evening your dog bit a piece out of the calf of my leg and I never noticed it until I got home."

A young botanist was showing his bride around the greenhouse.

"Now, dear, this flower belongs to the Dahlia family."

"I see," his love replied. "And you're keeping it for them while they're on vacation?"

"I want accommodations for my wife and myself," said the honeymooner, trying to sound businesslike.

"Suite, sir?" asked the hotel clerk.

"Er —" groped the bridegroom, blushing violently, "perfect!"

The little bride sadly informed her husband that there was no dessert for supper.

"I planned to have some sponge cake, dear, but it came out all funny."

"How come?" asked her husband, who was fond of sponge cake.

"I don't know," she said. "I guess maybe the store sent me the wrong kind of sponges."

Inscription on a cigarette lighter: "To My Matchless Wife."

"How are you doing in your new apartment?"

"Just fine. We furnished one of the three rooms with cigarette coupons."

"How about the other two?"

"Those — oh, well, they're full of cigarettes."

A truly charmed marriage is one in which a woman gives the best years of her life to the man who made them the best.

One Kentuckian was explaining to another how his sister had found a husband.

"It seems she saw this fellow's picture on a 'Wanted' poster, and she offered $50 more for him than the Government did."

Elsie: "Sandy, you shouldn't let yourself get discouraged. After all, in this world there's a man for every girl and a girl for every man. You really can't beat that."

Sandy: "Oh, I don't want to beat it — only to get in on it!"

"Darling," ventured the little wife, "I dented the fender just the slightest bit. If you want to look at it, it's in the back seat."

The farmer's young bride was sometimes shocked at the words he used.

"Where did you learn such awful language?" she finally asked.

"Learn it, hell, my dear, it's a gift."

Cindy had just served her very first dinner as a fledgling wife.

"Now, dear," she proudly asked, "what will I get if I make you a dinner like that every night?"

"Well," her husband reluctantly allowed, "you might get my life insurance."

"Do you shrink from kissing?" inquired the shy young fellow.

"Why, if I did," exclaimed his date, "I'd surely be a pitiful pile of bones!"

"I promise you," he said severely, "the next time you contradict me, I'm going to kiss you."

"Oh, no, you're not!" she cried.

The newlyweds had just opened a joint bank account.

"The bank has returned your last check," said the husband grimly.

"Oh, marvelous," replied his smiling bride. "What should I buy with it next?"

A friend of the George Bernard Shaws tells of an evening spent with them. While G.B.S. told endless stories, Mrs. Shaw worked intently on her knitting. When asked, in a quiet aside, what she was knitting, Mrs. Shaw whispered,

"Oh, nothing, nothing at all. It's just that I've heard these stories of his two thousand times, and if I didn't do something with my hands, I'm afraid I'd choke him."

———◆———

An excited Army recruit asked his company commander for an immediate furlough, explaining that his wife was going to have a baby. Permission was granted, and the soldier was leaving, when his C.O. asked exactly when the baby was due.

"About nine months after I get home, sir," replied the recruit casually.

———◆———

"Can you imagine," whispered one wedding guest to another, "they've only known each other for two weeks!"

"Well," replied her friend, "it's certainly one way of getting acquainted."

41

A country lad was driving to the local fair with his girl when they passed a stand where fresh popcorn was being sold.

"My! Abner, ain't that nice?" exclaimed the girl.

"Ain't what nice?"

"Why, the popcorn — it smells so awfully good!"

"It does smell kind o' fine," drawled the youth. "I'll jest drive a little closer so you can get a better smell."

Uncle Fred was holding his nephew on his lap on the crowded trolley, when a very pretty young lady stepped aboard.

Nudging his nephew, Fred gallantly suggested, "My boy, why don't you get up and give the lady your seat?"

Jill found a lovely place under a tree and pointed it out to Jack.

"This is a delightful spot for a picnic."

"It must be, love," the gallant Jack replied. "Fifty million insects can't be wrong."

42

Social notes in the Winding River *Daily Gazette:*

1. At the Founding Fathers picnic Sunday, Mrs. Thompson won first prize in the ladies' rolling-pin throwing contest. She threw her pin ninety-nine yards.

2. Mr. Thompson won the one hundred-yard dash.

———————

Paul and Paula decided to include some fishing in their honeymoon trip. Paula was a novice, and after sitting quietly in the boat for several minutes, she asked, "Darling, how much did the blue and yellow thing cost?"

"Do you mean the float? Only about fifteen cents."

"Well, that's good — because mine just sank."

———————

"Young feller," said the farmer, "I ain't blind, and I reckon you been sparkin' my gal Susie a lot lately. Is it all on the square, or ain't it?"

"Nope," replied the lad, " 'Tain't. Mostly on the back porch, I guess."

"Henry, darling," said the blushing bride as the honeymooners drove up to the portico of the Ritz, "let's try to convince the hangers-on in the lobby that we've been married for ages."

"Okay, my love," said Henry dubiously. "But do you think you can carry four suitcases by yourself?"

A very young fellow asked a girl of the same age if she would marry him when they grew up.

"I'm very sorry," she primly replied, "but that is impossible. In my family we always marry relatives. My father married my mother, my grandfather married my grandmother, and even my uncle married my aunt."

Two co-eds, one from Vermont, the other from Virginia, were chatting over coffee.

"We might as well face it," sighed the girl from New England. "Men are all alike."

The lass from Virginia smiled and agreed, "Men are all Ah like, too."

44

When a rather well-to-do young man was married, a column-long story of the wedding appeared in the society section of the local paper. On the train for their honeymoon trip, the newlyweds wanted to conceal their new status, so the groom was very nonchalant when he handed their long tickets to the conductor.

The official read and read. Finally, he raised his voice so the entire car could hear and said,

"My friend, this is a very interesting account of your wedding, but where are your tickets?"

A lovely young girl was overheard to say, "What I really want is to be swept off my feet by someone I can dominate."

"Why won't you marry me?" he demanded. "There isn't anyone else, is there?"

"Oh, Oscar," she sighed, "there must be."

"Now listen here, daughter," exploded the father, "you can't marry that young pup. He doesn't make more than $50 a month."

"Oh, but Daddy," pleaded the girl, "a month flies by so fast when you're in love with each other."

Sally: "Did you ever catch your husband flirting?"

Sarah: "Yes; that's the very way I did catch him!"

"Oh, darling," wailed the young bride as she padded back into the bedroom, "I had wanted to give you breakfast in bed, but the Danish pastry is still frozen in the refrigerator!"

"That's perfectly all right, love," her husband replied, "we'll eat it frozen and then turn up the electric blanket."

"Did you ever do any public speaking?" asked one old farmer of another.

"Well, I did once propose to a girl in the country over a party line."

"Darling, I've finally decided on a name for the new baby. Let's call her Minerva!"

"Well," replied her dismayed but tactful husband, "that's a fine name. In fact, I used to know a lovely girl named Minerva, and that name will always evoke happy memories."

There was a brief silence.

"You know, love, perhaps Lucy is really a nicer name...."

———◆———

A young fellow was trying to impress his parents with his girl-friend's accomplishments.

"You mean she can really speak three languages?" asked Mama.

"Yes! Manhattan, Bronx, and Brooklyn!"

———◆———

Sally and Carrie were bewailing their single state.

"At least I was two-thirds married once," Sally sighed. "I was there, and the Justice of the Peace was there, but the man didn't show up!"

48

After repeatedly assuring his bride that she "needn't be an expert" to play bridge with him and another couple, Charley finally overcame her hesitancy.

"I'll play," she agreed, "but I must warn you that I'm not awfully good."

"Don't worry," Charley assured her. "None of us are experts either."

On the very first hand, three consecutive passes left the bidding strictly up to Charley's bride. She studied her hand carefully, looked quickly at her husband, and bid, "Two clovers."

A very shy fellow was seated at a formal dinner next to a young lady whom he secretly adored. He was so intent on finding something clever to say that he ate very little.

Finally he saw his chance when the girl turned to him and remarked, "What a small appetite you have, Mr. Jeffers!"

"To sit next to you," he eagerly replied, "would cause any man to lose his appetite!"

A young husband who spent most of his leisure time at the racetrack came home one evening to find his wife behaving very strangely.

Telephoning his doctor, he explained that his wife seemed to think she was a racehorse.

"She's snorting and whinnying and chomping on the grass out front, doctor."

"Probably her reaction to your endless talk about horse racing," hazarded the doctor. "Bring her right over and I'll examine her."

"O.K.," replied the husband. "I'll gallop her over right after supper."

———◆———

A young city girl was vacationing in the country and became friendly with a farmer boy. One evening as they were strolling across a pasture they saw a cow and a calf rubbing noses in the accepted bovine fashion.

"Ah," said the farmer boy, "that sight makes me want to do the same."

"Well, go ahead," said the girl. "It's your cow."

50

A young wife wanted to give her husband a special birthday present. Since he liked to take pictures, she decided to give him fifty flash bulbs.

Of course, she wanted them to be quite perfect, so before she carefully wrapped each in silver paper, she tested them by firing each of them off in her husband's camera.

———◆———

Cynthia had a fine gift idea for her husband. Knowing how deeply he cared about his golf game, she entered a pro shop and told the salesman, "I'd like a low handicap, please."

When the salesman seemed puzzled, she explained, "Yes, a low handicap — for my husband's birthday. He's always saying he'd like one."

———◆———

"Darling," said the impoverished young man, when the subject of marriage came up, "you know I love you, but marriage is—just impossible. Why, I couldn't keep a canary."

"Of course you could, dear," the girl declared firmly. "I just love them."

A very sedate grandmother was upset when her eighteen-year-old grand-daughter announced that she was going off for a picnic all day with one of her suitors.

"In my day no nice girl would think of traipsing off with a man unless she was engaged to him!" said Grandma.

"Oh, that's all right," confided the girl. "He's one of my fiancés."

———◆———

The Girl: "I won't marry until I find a man with the courage of a lion, the wisdom of Socrates, the wit of Mark Twain; he must be handsome as a Greek god but never conceited; he must be gallant as Sir Walter Raleigh, but—"

The Man: "How fortunate we met."

———◆———

Miss Catherine's evening prayer: "O Lord, I ask nothing for myself: but will you please send dear Mother a son-in-law?"

———◆———

The wise husband meets a marital crisis with a firm hand — full of candy and flowers.

A dashing young lover swore by the stars that his lady was the loveliest in all the world, and that he would have none other.

"Be mine, dear lady," he pleaded, "for if you refuse me, I shall die."

But she refused him, and fifty years later he did die.

"You, down there!" shouted Father from the head of the stairs. "It's two-thirty! Do you think you can stay all night?"

"Er, thank you, sir," said the callow lover. "But I'll have to phone home first."

"Have you a volume entitled, *Man, the Master of Woman?*" inquired the customer.

"Fiction counter to the left, sir," replied the salesgirl.

Said a Quaker spinster who was asked why she had never married, "It takes a mighty good husband to be better than none."

While recovering at a Navy hospital, a young soldier was composing a letter home to his wife. A kind-hearted nurse was taking down the note.

"The nurses here," he dictated, "are a rather plain lot."

"Why," exclaimed the nurse, "don't you think that's rather harsh?"

The soldier smiled and exclaimed, "Yes it is, but it will make my wife very happy."

"I really don't understand you, Jack. Monday you like beans. Tuesday you like beans. Wednesday you like beans. Now, all of a sudden, on Thursday you *don't* like beans!"

Natalie took over her friend's fourth grade class while the friend went on a honeymoon. Later, at a party, someone was about to introduce the groom to Natalie.

"Oh," he answered alertly, "I know Miss Stevens very well. As a matter of fact, she substituted for my wife during our honeymoon."

Evident pride shone in the young lady's face as she described her new escort.

"He's sort of a short, fat Valentino, only blond."

There was a pained yelp from the bathroom.

"What's the matter, dear?" asked the young wife.

"It's my razor blade," he cried. "It's dull. It won't cut at all."

"Why, that's strange," she called back. "Your beard can't possibly be tougher than my lead pencil."

"I hear your fiancée speaks Esperanto. Does she speak it fluently?"

"Like a native," replied the proud fellow.

"Of course I'm not married," she said saucily. "I'm nobody's fool."

"Then," he said hopefully, "will you be mine?"

"You accuse me of extravagance," the recent bride tearfully wailed, "but you are twice as bad."

"Now when did I ever make a useless purchase?" asked her outraged spouse.

"Well — there's that expensive fire extinguisher you bought last month. We've never used it once!"

A well-trained Navy recruit was observed retrieving a handkerchief dropped by a shapely WAVE lieutenant. He handed it to her with a sincere, "I think you dropped this, toots, sir."

Girl answering telephone: "Marie isn't in just now. This is her 111-pound, five-foot-three, blonde, blue-eyed sister."

Marie reassured her husband: "Of course I spend more than you make, love, but then — I have great confidence in you!"

Asked if he liked intellectual girls, he replied, "I like a girl with a good head on my shoulder."

A young couple entered a drugstore and asked for a potent new baby tonic.

"Here's one," said the druggist, "that I can promise will make your youngster husky, handsome, and happy."

"That's just what we want," enthused the young lady, "but who takes it — my husband or I?"

She: "Dearest, will you take Father apart and speak to him?"

He: "Darling, when he hears my income, I won't have to take him apart. He'll explode."

"Sammy, I want to ask you a question."

"Anything, darling."

"Tell me — if you had never met me would you have loved me just the same?"

"When did you first know that you loved me?"

"When I began to get mad at people who said you were brainless and homely."

Arriving home unexpectedly, Henry found his wife in the arms of his best friend.

"Well, I'm glad finally to have this out," exclaimed the friend. "I love your wife and want her for my own. Let's be gentlemen and settle this with a game of cards. Winner takes Emily. All right? Shall we play gin rummy?"

"Sounds fine to me," replied Henry. "But how about a penny a point just to make the game interesting?"

"There's that fellow that is always annoying Rosalie."

"Why, he's not even looking at her!"

"Yes, and that's what annoys her."

She: "I suppose all geniuses are conceited."

He: "Some of them, my pet — but I'm not!"

"Dearest, am I good enough for you?"

"No, but you're too good for any other girl."

"It's terrible," confessed the youth. "She's the most wonderful girl in the world. And when I finally found the courage to propose, she turned me down."

"Well, cheer up, old chap!" replied a friend. "A woman's 'no' may often turn out to mean 'yes'."

"I know," said the lad mournfully. "But this girl didn't say 'no.' She said, 'Aw, phooey'!"

———◆———

Notes passed between two third-graders:

"Dear Judee: I luv you. Do you luv me? Jimmy."

"Dear Jimmy: I do *not* love you. Love, Judy."

———◆———

Frannie loved to phone her new husband at his hardware store.

"Oh, George — do bring a rat-trap home today."

"But you have the one I brought home last week, dear."

"Yes, darling, but there's a rat in that."

61

Jessie was reporting eagerly to her husband on the behavior of their new neighbors.

"They seem to be a wonderfully happy couple. Why, every time he leaves, she comes to the door and he warmly embraces and kisses her. Wouldn't it be nice if you did that?"

"Why darling, I haven't even been introduced to her!"

An anxious young father-to-be, bringing his wife into the maternity ward asked, "Darling, are you sure that you want to go through with this?"

"I'm in love with you," sighed the patient. "I don't want to get well."

"You won't," replied his enchanting nurse. "The doctor saw you kissing me, and he's in love with me, too."

THE END!